WAKEFIELD PRESS

EVERY
TIME
YOU
CLOSE
YOUR
EYES

Bel Schenk is the author of the poetry
collections *Ambulances & Dreamers* and
Urban Squeeze. She lives in Melbourne.

'The inflections with which Bel Schenk greets that odd
couple, urban love and urban loneliness, are all her own.'
– J.M. Coetzee, on *Ambulances & Dreamers*

'There is a knowingness, an ambiguity at the heart of Schenk's
poetry that resists easy labels.' – Geoffrey Lehmann, *The Australian*

T0358127

EVERY TIME YOU CLOSE YOUR EYES

Wakefield
Press

BEL SCHENK

Wakefield Press
16 Rose Street
Mile End
South Australia 5031
www.wakefieldpress.com.au

First published 2014

Cover designed by Liz Nicholson, designBITE
Text designed by Ryan Paine
Typeset by Clinton Ellicott, Wakefield Press
Printed in Australia by Griffin Digital, Adelaide

National Library of Australia Cataloguing-in-Publication entry

Author: Schenk, Bel, author.
Title: Every time you close your eyes / Bel Schenk.
ISBN: 978 1 74305 319 5 (paperback).
Subjects: Australian poetry.
Dewey Number   A821.4

Government
of South Australia
Arts SA

fox creek
wines

Australian Government

Publication of this book was assisted by
the Commonwealth Government through the
Australia Council, its arts funding and advisory body.

For Rachel

Every Time You Close Your Eyes is set during the North American blackouts of 1977 and 2003. All of the characters are fictional except for David Berkowitz and Christopher Reeve. David Berkowitz, also known as Son of Sam, is an American serial killer and arsonist. His crimes terrorised New York City from July 1976 until his arrest in August 1977. Christopher Reeve played Superman in four movies. He was paralysed from the neck down after a horse riding accident in 1995 and died in 2004.

Contents

Part 1

New York City – Summer, 1977 2

Fade 3

Ammunition 4

Television Flickers 5

The Subway System 6

The Soldiers 7

The Shop Owner vs The Looters 8

Hiding 9

Superman 10

Embrace 11

After the Shopping Spree 12

They Evacuate the Art Show 14

Dear Sam, ... 16

Romance 17

42 Pine Street 18

Misbehaving 19

Full Breakfasts and Strong Coffee 21

Questions for the Survey 23

The Disco 26

Inhale to Exhale 27

Falling Star 29

Afterwards, They Share a Drink   30

Comic Book   31

Her Walk   32

War Games   33

Light   34

Inventory, 1977   35

Part 2

New York City – Summer, 2003   38

Aviation   39

Alex   41

Twelve Million Text Messages   42

Subway Operators   43

Upgrade   45

Robert   46

The Airport   47

The Way You Spin It   48

Memory   49

You Said Something   50

Dent   51

The Butcher Cooks His Meat Before It Spoils   52

Martha Flicks a Smile at Alex   53

Things Like Climbing   54

Grip   55

Multiple Choice   56

The Traffic Controller   57

The Night   59

The Height of Buildings   60

Exactly   61

Everyone Has a Story . . .   62
Offline   63
Alex   64
Passing   65
Weightless   66
What This Feels Like   67
On Top of the Ferris Wheel   68
Alex   69
Catch Me as I Fly Over This Horse   71
Quietly Dizzy   72
Break   73
The Day   74
About a Bridge   75
In Camera   76
Game   77
Strings Attached   78
Alex Takes It On   79
Questions   80
Inventory, 2003   81
Epilogue   83

Notes From the Author   85

PART 1

New York City
Summer, 1977

The lights go out just before dark.
There is a blackout in the city
and people blame lightning.
There are many different ways to tell this story.

This is one of them.

Fade

The crash of glass on one small man's head.
He lies bleeding in the gutter.

His fingers form a fist, clutching,
as if holding a weapon

or someone's hand. People walk on, unwilling to bend.
Only one person calls out.

The final repeat of the echo fades
and darkness is set to tumble through.

Ammunition

Three and a half blocks away, through alleys
and streets, but still, this is Brooklyn.
Here, a boy and his bed. One hides under the other.
Soon, but not yet, he will fall
into a complicated sleep.

His soldiers drive army tanks and carry plastic guns.
The boy's flashlight shines a path ahead.
Whether he hears shooting, imagined or real,
he'll never know. If he does, it's best to pretend
that it comes from the tiny weapons of toys.

Television Flickers

Out on the street, the flicker of television screens dissolve
through apartment windows. Robert searches for candles
and matches to direct him through the long hours of night.

To the left, next door and below, the barman locks the doors.
Men knock on them, loud, as if they might open to a more
petulant beat. Seventeen types of vodka rattle on the shelves.

Should the men rest their mouths below and wait
for a bottle to spill and drizzle over them? Here in this state,
someone will mumble. Somebody will say: *You are wonderful.*

The Subway System

People on the platform recall the location
of the exit light's glow and follow the sound
and energy made by the movements of others.
If you're a reliable sort you give directions
to anyone who will follow and anyone who will trust.
The rats are hushed.
There seems no need to scurry under the railings.
The A train is somewhere under the city.

There, deep beneath earth and concrete,
under grass and overhead footsteps,
people are stuck inside the carriage.
They hold things, feel their dirty way.
Shit, yes, it's dark. No sir, you can't see. You can't see.
Inside the people, blood rises and falls,
breathing grows faster. Shallow.
Deep inside is exactly what you are thinking right now.

The Soldiers

They won't save him. After all, they are toys.
Sure, he can imagine. Of course he can imagine.
He can make shooting sounds with his mouth
and create as much blood as he needs. Some time soon,
he'll have to come out for something to eat.
The soldiers won't feed him.
They might not even be on his side.

The Shop Owner vs The Looters
(an uneven contest)

They come at nightfall. From behind the counter
the shop owner shouts and swings his fists to conduct them out.
They grunt as they punch things and run through his aisles.
Boxes fall, breaking objects inside.

Coffee. Smashed glass mixes with blood.
Tea, Sugar cubes, breakfast items.
The smell of fire from outside.

A gun fires through a Warhol soup tin.
Someone screams: *Fire, police, fire.*
Police are coming. Tomato soup, as shiny as blood,
but paler in shade.

And the shop owner, he's down in aisle two
after whack in the jaw and ten counts.
You could have stayed behind the counter. Waited it out.
You could have been a contender.

Someone has lost it.
Someone's banged up and bruised
flipping on the lino floor. The shop sells bandaids
but not for this kind of cut.

In aisle five, the box for this smashed up transistor radio reads:
Batteries not included.

Hiding

Here comes the boy, out from under the bed
His face is creased with carpet grooves
and close by, in the next room, his mother cleans.
Call it hunger, call it fear, call it loneliness,
he meets her in the kitchen.
She makes him cheese on white bread,
cut into quarters. She pats his head and bends down
to kiss his cheek. Pulls him close and wraps her arms
around him. She sits him on the bench
and tells him to not be afraid of the dark.

Sometimes when you imagine hard enough
you can confuse make believe
with memory. It happens
sometimes. If you try.

Superman

Where is Superman when you need him?
Memorising lines? Wondering if this
is the beginning or perhaps the end of his career?

No, he's all the way up, looking down and across blunt buildings,
waiting for the crew to bring him down.

On a crane, high over Manhattan,
Christopher Reeve is stuck in the sky.
He is about to be a star. You can just tell with some people.
They've either got it or they don't.

Just his luck he's wearing full body spandex.
Rumour has it the tech crew plugged in too much power
and destroyed a gigantic metropolis in one hit.

Yes, Superman is up there, up high,
somewhere between flying and falling.

Embrace

Robert's cello sits tall in his apartment.
His strings are tuned and the maple wood polished.
The curves are like a line of music. A verse of song.
Outside, listen: the shouts and the screams
land in higher places. He sits behind and throws his arms around
the wood and drowns the voices with those long strokes.
Curves a line of music. A verse of song.
When he plays, the woman above
lowers her eyes as she listens to the notes
glide over the guts of the cat.
Closer, she puts her ear to the floor
and waits there, until the end of the last bar,
repeating like waves.

After the Shopping Spree

From broken shop-front windows,
boxes are tossed from man to
man from the south side to the
alleyway. Alarms fail. Even the
sirens can't make their point
clear enough.

Police stations always seem to
be downtown. Wherever this
one stands, there's not enough
room for all the people here.
Some refuse to talk. Some fight.
Some cry. In the cells, there's
shouting: *Fuck you, man! Lemme
outta here. I ain't done nothin'
wrong? Everyone's doin' it.*

It's hot outside. Hearts jolt.
Men carry boxes from cars and
up flights of stairs, each thigh
muscle stuffed into tight flared
jeans. Dry mouths splashed with
water or a mouthful of coke.

In the cells, there's calming: *Be quiet. Nothing's gonna get done with all this noise. Just stay quiet.* Advice: *Why don't you try gettin' the real criminals, huh? Son of Sam's probably killing some lady right now. Psycho serial-killing freak!*

Someone follows someone else, panting faster. He holds on to what he's got between his arms. It doesn't matter what it is. Faster and stronger with this broken thing. The sweat on his face beaming, he heads back again for a second turn.

But what they really notice is the stench of sweat as they're thrown in. No phone calls allowed, some ask others what their problem is. And since you haven't spoken to her for three months and one week, what would you say anyway?

I love you. I'm sorry. I'm in trouble.
Come get me? Baby? I'm sorry.
It's dark.

They Evacuate the Art Show

Outside the gallery, you look for her on the curb.
You want to tell her something. You need her to know.

You swerve with a tray of champagne in your hands.
The room is full of artists and students.
She takes a glass and you want to say:
You have the straightest back I have ever seen.
You say it and the words fold into each other
like a note between pages. She doesn't hear you.
You watch her fingers on the stem of the glass. She looks at you
and you try to slip inside the hoods of her eyes.
Tuck yourself in and float on the glimmer.
People scamper out. You place the palm of your hand
on the small of her back to usher her out.
Trick yourself into thinking it's part of your job.
She has the straightest back you have ever touched.

People on the street mill about and chatter.
You carry the bucket of ice and bottles to the crowd
and pop them all. Throw ice in the air and let bubbles
fall to the ground. It feels like rain.
You say it again, this time, under your breath.
You have the straightest back I have ever seen.
The words merge with the speed of the bustle

as you try to find her. Somewhere. Down the street.
There. Yes, you freeze her there.
There. There she goes.

Dear Sam,

Ma says I will grow out of soldiers and also my lisp. It is because my teeth are crooked at the front. I sometimes see things about you on the news. People saying stay home at night. I will stay home at night. I am only nine. I know why soldiers kill people. It is because they have to or else they will get in trouble. Will you get in trouble if you don't kill people? Before he left, my Pa told me that I had to protect my Ma. I will. But she is not scared of you. She is not scared of anything. I sometimes wish that blankets were cold in the summertime so I could snuggle up without getting hot. I hope you get this letter. I do not know where to send it.

Romance

Bernie comes down to her.
I can't be out for too long, Rosie.
I told her I was getting supplies so I better get back with supplies.
Batteries. A torch. Cans. Is that the kind of thing people need?
How long will this last for, do you think?

They take the car. How long can this last for?
We're not supposed to be out tonight.
They park at the river's edge
and the Twin Towers – black skinny trousers
stand on the edge of Manhattan.
Tonight, only headlights from cars and trucks
shine pretty on the water.

42 Pine Street

Police: Let me haunt you with these words: I'll be back! I'll be back! To be
interpreted as – bang bang bang, bank, bang – ugh!!
Yours in murder.
From a hand-written letter, written by serial killer David Berkowitz,
otherwise known as Son of Sam.

In Apartment 7E, David wonders whether to head out or stay in.
The view of the Hudson River
with its steady stream of navy offers no direction.

His dog has been talking in strange phrases. Odd ways.
It's as if he is in control. David opens a pack of peas
and eats them frozen. Once, there was a steady line to continue on.
A path with an easy tread.

Now, when he is most expected, he stays in.
The dog makes it clear after he drinks again,
from the un-flushed toilet bowl.

Misbehaving

1. The boy dares to look outside.
Containers of food burn near the deli down the street.
A man runs, collecting people on the way.

2. Never leave the apartment at night.
He has been told.

3. A piece of cardboard keeps the apartment door ajar.
He climbs to the rooftop.
Never leave the apartment at night.

4. The tops of his teeth bite the lower lip
to stop the shakes. The crash of Brooklyn.
Women roam and men steal.

5. And his mother . . .
He does not yell for her.
He does not yell.

6. A man and a woman
from somewhere
ask what he's doing.
He says: *Nothing much, just looking.* They step closer:
Do you want to come and talk to us? We live here too.

7. He does not yell for her.
He does not yell.

8. *What number are you in?*
We locked ourselves out.
What a night to lock ourselves out.

9. I hope you got the letter, Sam.
I did not know where to send it.

10. The man steps close.

11. The boy jumps back. He does not yell for her.
The man in overalls whistles a tune. There is stubble on his face
and a stench, odd. Grease.

12. If the boy runs at a pace of nine miles per hour
how long does it take him to climb back down those stairs?

13. Swiftly. That's how long.
He outruns them. His body swerves and weaves.
His tiny legs lead him back down.

14. How fast he runs.
How they shout: *Come back, let us in.*

Full Breakfasts and Strong Coffee

Yesterday.
At 5.30 Rose wakes with her arms wrapped
around a sideways pillow. Weekdays she's at work by 6
– lipstick, an apron, comfortable shoes –
then at 8, a break to make sure the boy is up and ready for school
– cereal, juice, science books.

For the big tips, she smiles as wide as her mouth can stretch
and remembers to wiggle her hips
when taking the orders to the kitchen.

This man on television above the counter.
6'4, dark hair, blue eyes. Christopher Reeve.
She watches him make bad choices
on the soap opera – *Love of Life* –
all of the drama Rose might have
if she plays it right.

Another waitress tells her he's filming that Superman movie.
You should find him. Just yesterday they were filming on 43rd.
It's time you got out there again, anyway. You deserve it.

Rose deserves it. Clark Kent and blue eyes.
The Superhero, the reporter and the soap star
all rolled into one good man. One good man.

Her heart glides over the smell of full breakfasts
and strong, bottomless coffee.
Her heart glides like a rescued Lois Lane.

Questions for the Survey

In the halls of the high school,
the cleaner wheels his tools down slippery floors,
past lockers and dozens of messages in black on the walls.

A student carrying out a survey about safety
carries a clipboard and a pen:

If you had an accident – were unconscious –
would the person who found you know who to call?

I don't know.

It's really a good idea to carry some kind of card
showing your next of kin.
Just in case, you know?

Yep. Sure thing.

Have you ever had an experience
that has made you realise your mortality?

Is this a question for your survey?

Yes.

I realise it every day.

Are you going home to a living situation of (please pick one)
1 person
2 people
3 people
4 people
Other.

Is this a question for your survey?

No.

Other. None. Just me.

Does the staff room have beer in the fridge?

Is this a question for your survey?

No.

I think so.

Is the beer getting warm? This is not a question for my survey.

Yes.

Do you drink alcohol (pick one):
Never

Occasionally
Only socially
Frequently
Daily

Is this a . . .

No.

Socially. Only socially. Best change that to occasionally.
In staffrooms.

Warm beer occasionally in deserted staffrooms.

Has anyone ever cried over you?

Is this a question for your survey?

No. But I am interested to know.

Let's go kid. Let's go and drink beer.
I have all of the keys to this place.

The Disco

Even without the mirror balls and the sounds,
people dance. Remembering how to feel,
they carry the beat and the rhythm with them.
A syncopated bass line runs through.

This girl on the floor,
kicking and spinning and completely shiny.
She is like the moon.
To all the empty spaces, she gives a glow.

Inhale to Exhale

In the backseat the leather sticks.
Rose sits, her dress hitched around her waist.
Bernie's buckle is undone. Shoes remain tied to his feet.
She lies back, her head against the window.
What was that noise? she whispers.
Relax, Rosie. You're too tense tonight.

He peels off her underwear.
Her high heels land with the coins
and dust under the seats.

Streets away, Robert plays cello in a murky room.
The chords long through his arms
and strong between his legs.
The notes stop in the sticky air outside.
They'll never reach any ears on the street.

The boy slams his apartment door. Scares a cat outside.
It jumps from the fire escape to the alleyway.
On its paws, the grease leaves a trail.

Back in the car, they shove and shift.
The sweat rolling in between them as they move.
The exquisite sadness of a sonata.
Back beats in alleys.
Claws. Violent peaks. Breathing and timing.

The last note is played. The cat stops running.
Bernie ejaculates.
Fuck. Baby. I need supplies.

The cat chases a rat into the gutter.
The boy locks the door, his back and a pile of things sit against it.
He counts how long he can hold his breath
as his face gets redder and redder. He does not call for her.
He does not call.

The cello set down.
Robert holds a mouthful of whiskey on the back of his tongue
before he swallows.

Rose puts her hand to her cheek
and feels the flush and flurry. Redder and redder.
For a second of deep and warm,
they all hold their breath and again, sigh it out.

Falling Star

On the square of grass near his place
Robert might get some fresh air.
A foolish thought.

The needles on the ground are tough to see
so he feels his space and lies down.
In this park, people continue to earn a living.

A bus passes through the street
and a boy surfs on the roof, shouts: *Take me to the moon.*
Robert wonders if all the birds are sleeping.

People in cities often forget to look up.
Robert sees a falling star for the first time
and remembers someone he used to know.

If only he were here to see that.

Afterwards, They Share a Drink

The shop owner sells supplies for seven times their value.
He can. There is demand.
He has a gun and a bruise swelling darker on his chin.
Rose stands aside. Mascara and lipstick smudged on her cheeks.
She wants a drink. Demand. He has a gun. This is backwards.

The cops ain't doing nothin' to protect us, man. We gotta take control.
You want these things, man, you pay for 'em.
I lost half my shit tonight.
And you, lady, don't you know there's a maniac on the loose.
Killing people. In car seats!

Rose knows. She wants a drink. She wants a martini
on a kitchen bench as Bernie rides her dress up past her hips
and bites her neck. But she'll take a beer.
She'll take anything she can.

Bernie throws a twenty at the shop owner.
Smiles: *Keep the change.*
And Rose? *Babe, I'm late. I gotta leave you here. You okay to walk?*

Comic Book

With his flashlight,
the boy reads the *Superman* comics
he's piled against his door. This makes him,
for a moment, brave.

If the floor creaks in the hallway, even a little,
he'll feel it. He'll be ready.
The boy sees the world in lines and panels,
in heroes and villains.

He'll be ready. The skin under
his nails bleeds. The pressure on his bladder
builds and releases . . .
releases.

Her Walk

Rose's best companion is her walk.
She takes it everywhere. Past buildings
and dark avenues.

She might like to quicken pace when she passes the men,
but she strides with high heeled precision, avoiding the pot holes
on the pavement. Convincing herself she's fearless.

Convincing herself of many things:
Love. The boy, asleep.

From piles of sneakers dumped on street corners
men find pairs in any size.

War Games

The laundry basket with its piles of clothes.
The boy finds last week's pyjamas
and replaces them. They are not his favourite
but they are dry. He waits for the sound of a key in the door.
Tiny soldiers line up ready to attack.
A tank parks next to them. Heavy and big.
She has to get past all of this, this whole army
before she can check if he is alright.
All of it. Ready. Aim.

At 2am he gives up and falls asleep.
Rose struggles into her doorway.
She picks him up and carries him to bed.
The feeling of floating when he wakes.
She's home and she smells like his memory.
Are the lights back, Ma?

No, Alex, sweetheart, they're still out.
I'll make you pancakes in the morning.

She puts him to bed.
When she lies down beside him
he curls into her familiar grooves.

Light

Someone gets it first.
It returns like dominos clacking through the city.
In reverse. Even fish swimming in aquariums
notice the return of mechanical bubbles pushing to the surface.
The shop owner emerges
with an aftertaste of ridiculous disarray.
Every time he closes his eyes
he will feel the difference
between before and after.

Inventory, 1977

In the end, darkness or light, things remain.
Food is chucked or eaten today.
News reporters churn out numbers and advice.

The people in the know
say the energy system is fundamentally flawed.
Reports are written and articles are read.

Some still believe that bolts of lightning
pumped the sky with straight and diagonal lines
like the last five letters of the alphabet.

Some didn't notice at all.
They slept through it or lived like usual, in the dark.
They took cues from their dogs and stayed.

One person sang *Puff the Magic Dragon* for three hours straight.
One person hugged a stranger and lingered for too long.
3,776 people were arrested, generating heat in cells.

One person forgave her, almost.
At times he's reminded, at very odd times,
such as watching the Oscars and eating ice cream.

Someone jumped higher then he ever had before
and decided to take up jumping as a sport.
Someone claimed to have turned the switch off from outer space.

One person hid in alleyways, shouting boo to anyone.
He still keeps the coat he wore.
His kids take it out for dress ups.

Three people fell in love.
Some 26 years later, two of them have fallen out of it.
One remains.

He is whispering thoughts through the city.

PART 2

New York City
Summer, 2003

The lights go out at 4.30pm
and people pray it is only lightning.

Are you still here?
This will not be a repeat of before.

Aviation

The aerial shot from the single-engine Cessna
as it flies over the city.
Radio sounds travel from pilot to passengers
as they look below.

Since '77 new towers have been built
and others have fallen,
some with the people inside of them still.

So much has been eaten and drunk.
The ones still standing are full of beer, wine, cigars and food.
Each grain of rice boiled.
Billions. So many to count.

Bodies float, some in the river, others in hotel pools.
Movie stars and poets buy on 88th,
now famous because they live here.
Everyone knows.

And it's not just the towers and the planes.
It's the money and the politics and the way people talk.
In the village, a rock star shot.
Trees planted. City squares between streets cleaned out.
Art hanging in a swirling gallery.
A bomb and sex scandals – newspapers sell.
Greedy trade in the leather of a briefcase.
Four hundred thousand people marching against a war.

The blizzard of '96 and the blackout of '77
remembered differently, recorded all the same.
Here is a grid. To continue this city, insert activity.

Alex

Architects talk about gravity.
Alex entertains the idea that he would jump
rather than burn.

Architects sit in open plan.
Listen to talk radio
and watch clocks.

The electricity fails.
Computer screens fade to black.
Architects sigh and begin to make bigger plans.

Twelve Million Text Messages

With the overused network, some reach their destination
and others find random and confused readers.
Some never make it down.
They stay climbing
elsewhere and upwards.
And some cheeky ones
land on the phone screens
of lonely people
they were never meant for.

Where are you?

Subway Operators

Calm, trained voices
soothe worried passengers.
Some soften their foreign accents.

It is dark, pitch black
but they can smell the person
sitting next to them.

Martha can taste beef on the man's breath
and moth balls from his shirt.

There will be directions to follow soon.
The man leans over to Martha:
Take my hand, he says,
it is too dark.

At first, she refuses,
thinking sleaze,
of men in crowded bars
offering drinks with obligation.

But she selects the appropriate grip
over three calluses
and places immediate trust
in the hands of the classical cellist.

One by one, they move to the front carriage.
The only exit door.
Martha hears another man behind: *Hurry up.*

Walk in front of someone faster than you
and you're always off balance.
Their shoes always seem to be in between your feet.

Still, he's behind her: *Hurry the fuck up.*
Fuck off she says back.
I fucking wish that I could.
I fucking wish that you could too, freak show.

When trapped underground, it's important
to trust your instincts and listen.
Look for the light and the sounds of streets,
horns and people and all of their thoughts
both spoken and withheld.
Find sunglasses when you reach the street.
They are there in her jeans.
The light has never been so bright.

Upgrade

Sometimes taking the stairs down
feels harder than climbing up.
It's to do with balance and creaky kneecaps.
Thirty-something kneecaps. This used to be easy.

Alex makes sure people from every floor
get down with a minimum of hassle.
A girl from accounts asks if he'd like to grab a beer.
He tells her he needs to work out what this is all about.
Thanks though. I would have loved to.

His boss runs down three steps at once:
Alex get your ass out.
Someone asks if anything crashed up there.
Theories emerge, but right now, it's all hot air.

Robert

He asks her if she is okay. She says yes.
And you sir? Do you need anything?
I'll be alright.
He buys a black coffee and a litre of water
from the vendor and brushes the dust from his suit.
Starts walking.

Lines of people wait for the telephone
and stubbornness equates to crankiness
when someone dares to touch another man.
People make plans to meet.
They say they're going to be hours.
The line gets longer and longer.

Robert looks back.
There's always an upside
at having no one to call.

The Airport

Passengers panic at the slightest difference.
Staff refuse to think they make judgements
based on accents or family names.
The large voice on the PA makes it clear
that there's no flying out,
or in
or over.
For the toll free number of the airline
call: 1800-555-3761.
In the lounge, a plump man slumps in a row of blue seats
and watches jet planes tortoise on the tarmac.

The Way You Spin It

Robert walks into a bar he used to drink at.
The posters on the wall advertise the latest bands
and the coolest new drinks around.
The man at the bar pads down a coaster
and Robert orders a whiskey, *no make that a beer.*
This place has changed a lot since I used to come here.

He falls into 1977 like it's written in italics.
The emphasised past. *It stands out.* Demands attention.
There's a way to feel things more clearly.
Through photos and songs and triggers.
Today, under the sound of cars,
sit the delicate voices of children playing in the street
as if it's the day before the beginning of school.
From the bar window, all too aware of the complications
of such an act, he tracks the baseball
with the eye of a spectator waiting for the winning home run.
Caught out, the boy sits in the gutter.
Shoulders slouched. Eyes cast down.
There are ways to feel better about lack of physical ability.
Blame this heat. The way the sun sits in the sky
like it's plotting your downfall.
There are ways to feel better about most things.
Blank spaces and pauses. Italics deleted.
Washing the dirt from your cut knee.
It's all in the way you spin it.
It's all in the way the italics curve.

Memory

Soldiers and disco dresses.
An unlikely combination
yet strangely, Alex ponders,
a dead hot mix.

You Said Something

To a song from a battery powered stereo
three guys dance in a circle
and sing of rooftops in Brooklyn at one in the morning.
Lights flashing in Manhattan:
You said something
that I've never forgotten.

The tall one swings over to Robert:
Hey man, come and dance with us?

You want me to dance?

The one in blue, closer: *Sure, if you can?*

Robert slides from his stool and starts to click his fingers,
a pattern to go with the song.
Joins the circle, hips sway and the guys still sing:
You said something
that was really important.

Sing some more. Take hold of my breath, he thinks.
Wipe my sweat and tell me where the lights are going tonight.

Dent

Alex stands on the concrete
and looks up at the huge double-glazed
and streaked window pane
through which, on weekday mornings,
lunches and afternoons
he has stared south,
to the tug boats on the water
and to the big dusty crater
dented into the city.

I'm sitting in a subway
carriage. All I can
think about is you and
how I should have
stayed last night. All I
can say over and over
is I love you I love you
I love you.

The Butcher Cooks His Meat Before It Spoils

Boys come from around the corner
and from underground to fill bags and plates for home.

The sausages fry on gas heat.
People wrap them in bread, mustard and onions.
The vegetarians revisit moral choices
and the butcher trades his profit for dozens of smiles.

Barking dogs try to break from their leads
and Alex takes his phone out to call Rose.
Martha passes him a hotdog.

His phone, dead now, back in his satchel.
He takes food from a stranger
and finds a reason to eat when already full.

Hey everyone. Come
to mine. I have beer
and cold cuts. Get
here anyway you can.
Otherwise, see you on
the other side.

Martha Flicks a Smile at Alex

He is suddenly the tallest, the strongest
and the best looking kid on the team.
The quarterback with the muscles.
The dude at the party with the keg.
She says he looks hungry.
He admits that he's not feeling so great. A little faint.
Where are you headed? she asks.
Brooklyn he says and she says: *Snap*
and they walk. Slower than usual.
Men play drums nearby,
hands beat down on tight leather.
Alex makes sure they are walking in time.
If nothing else, he's careful not to miss a beat.

Things Like Climbing

The only way up
when the elevator is down,
is one at a time. Slowly.

Or by using corny circus tricks
as transport. Flying upwards with the wind
from the ground to 919.
A catapult. Rose imagines a catapult.

At age 58
It might be better to wait
at the bottom with dreams of a superhero.

There are things to worry about now,
like the pot roast on the bench
the plot twist on the show
and about silence.

The hum of the fridge absent.
A reminder of things never noticed
until they're gone.

Grip

Walk across the bridge.
To not lose each other
hold hands. Grip.

Home is a taxi ride away
or a long walk on bitumen
that sticks to old sandals.

Over the edge
rubbish floats or sinks
depending on its weight.

It's as if all these walkers
are taking a pilgrimage to somewhere.
Or escaping another place.

Let go to open the top of a cola bottle.
The plastic rips and the effervescence releases a low *shhhhhh*
like grumpy parents in movie theatres.

Disguise a sigh of frustration through a burp of bubbles.
Throw plastic from railings.
Wonder if it sinks or swims.
Hold hands again.

Multiple Choice

Alex waits as Martha ties her sneakers
and thinks that this could be a good time to:

A)
Walk, alone, in the opposite direction.
The Cowboy in the Sunset
not glancing back.

B)
Ask, ever so casually,
if she'd like to get a drink.
Just one, for the heat.

C)
Extend a hand
to see if she'd shake it goodbye
or hold on.

Don't be surprised if
I say something silly
today.

The Traffic Controller

There is an art to directing traffic.
You can learn it, but the beauty
has to come naturally.

Robert knows this.
He is blessed with grace, perspective
and outstanding eyesight.

A basic need to silence the
horns and separate the bumper bars
on the naughts and crosses grid of Manhattan.

And so it goes that when he steps out from the bar
and onto the road with his arms stretched, cars stop and go.
The mess and confusion restored, for a time.

After a little while of directing,
tiredness comes into the mix
and a police officer asks him to move along.

As he walks, street numbers grow larger,
his lungs smaller, and the breeze keeps stopping
when he most needs to breathe it in.

Despite all of this Robert makes it home.

Finds the rhythm as he walks.

In his absence, traffic crashes.

The Night

At last the sun goes down.
People get set for a night that wraps
the city with its enormous sheet.
Most manage to keep their spirits high.
Some weep into it.

The Height of Buildings

Street signs send people in wrong directions.
Clocks stop. Painters paint. Dogs bark.
Alex and Martha cut down a laneway to a bar,
climb stairs past kids on the fire escape
smoking cigarettes and joints.
The illuminated messages on billboards disappear.
Products become un-buyable.

One of the kids says to Martha: *No rules tonight.*
She nods: *About time.*
The kids climb higher. The even paced footsteps
on the metal ladder waltz upwards.
Inhaled by the height of buildings.

You have the
straightest back I have
ever seen

Exactly

Suddenly it is romance
in the restaurant
as the waiter brings candles
and fills glasses with wine.

The woman says:
Do you find it odd
that I prefer to sit next to you
rather than opposite?

On this night, the paintings behind them look deeper,
more abstract in this new light.
The shop owner tells her about before,
nightmares and sleep
and how his jaw has never been the same.

He takes her hand and tells her:
I love you. I really do.

Meeting his gaze she manages:
Me too.

Something similar,
but not exact.

Everyone Has a Story . . .

about the planes in the towers. Alex asks.
Martha says there was a guy she used to go to school with
in Tower: *He flew. Then fell. I liked him. He died. Sad.*

He died. Sad.

And it all comes down to a line
in a children's book.
Like this is all there is left. Sad.

And you, Alex? You knew anyone?

No. I didn't.
Sad in itself right?

Let's just Thank God this isn't the same.

Which God are you talking about?

And just like that – boom –
they enter religion.

Offline

Rose's computer has 34 percent power and zero connection.
She opens photographs she's saved
and profiles she's pasted to her desktop.
Studies them again and marks them from one to ten.

Glass of wine, peanuts,
she types a reply to send tomorrow:

It's my first time too! Who would have thought I'd be doing it.
My son (adult – don't worry) helped set up my profile, but to be honest
I haven't wanted to meet anyone. Until now that is . . .

Saved, she pours another glass.

Alex's voicemail.

Alex

(In the stairwell, she fell)

In the stairwell, she fell,
ankle bent and bruised.
I carried her weight.
Her breath against my neck.
She whispered: *Don't drop me*
like a lover might say:
Take over. Hold me everywhere.
We were shapeless,
counting steps down each numbered floor.
Moving like madness.

Passing

Robert lies awake glassy with memories.
He once meant to tell someone
that he thought darkness and emptiness
were alike. And tonight, as every hour passes
unchanged, his body flat on the mattress,
he is still here recalling someone's breath and heartbeat
shallow and quiet.

Breath and heartbeat. He had once said
that you can't have one without the other,
and he was exquisite that night, in the way he said it.
And in the way the back
of his hand moved on Robert's chest
up and down
up and down.
Quenching his thirst for surface.

Weightless

Outside, sweat falls from Martha's nose.
She inhales and says: *I feel awake.*
Alex holds his breath for thirteen seconds
and feels light. This woman limping next to him,
this awake woman,
lets him feel weightless.

And from space
the satellites continue to take pictures
for surveillance.
Alex and Martha kiss,
the tops of their heads concealed
by darkness. Both of them,
rushing their breath. Thinking –
trying to remember
what *this* feels like.

What This Feels Like

Puffed-out and dizzy from climbing
they reach the top floor, just before the entrance to his place.
Soles feel the path to the door. She limps there.
Another excuse to hold her close.

A neighbour sings opera
imported from elsewhere.
For spaghetti from home
and smooth lullabies,

there is sudden nostalgia
for the old Brooklyn apartment.
An urge to phone
the warm maternal voice,

to visit memories
of hands patting to sleep
the boy with the scruffed hair
and the most wonderful insomnia.

Hey, are you in
power? We're out.

On Top of the Ferris Wheel

It feels like freedom, a contradiction.
There's something about the cage they are in.
Stopped at the peak, these two, and apart from the jerking
of their own bodies, there is no momentum.

Freedom, or a fantasy. The way a child never wants
the amusement park ride to end.
The grin and the screams.
The happy fear. She says: *I never want to come down.*

The cogs of the machine
as the back up generator turns.
It's over now.
Why is this the scariest part? I could be here forever.

Alex

In the kitchen, we drink large glasses of water
and I begin to undress you.
Your perspiration shines in the groove
where your neck ends and the top of your ribs begin.
I run my hands along the back of your shirt,
a mix of the grit from the subway,
white cotton, and grease – the buttons are small.
Turning an opened eye into the cheekiness of a wink,
I undo all ten of them. Your shirt slides from your shoulders,
inside out, along your arms, over your wrists
and lands on the kitchen floor. I had imagined this once.
One morning, months before.
It doesn't matter where it lands exactly,
as long as it steadily falls
onto the tops of our feet.

I have undressed women before you
but it has been fuelled by music or lighting
and everything that goes with knowing somebody. I swear,
I am awake but empty to details of you.

I kiss your forehead. Counting the seconds it takes
to reach your mouth –
three, four, five.
There's a stillness about your face,
a questioning look in your eyes that says *when*
rather than *why*. I like the word *wanting*.

Then I kiss the tiny freckle on your neck.
It's like licking the last crumb from the plate
where a delicious meal once waited. It's time.
I count three, four, five, six, seven.

Sometimes there are things to record.
Later, when you're a little less close.
As if an anecdote adapted for canvas.

Catch Me as I Fly Over This Horse

Eight years after he took off from the saddle,
flying, for once, actually flying,
crashing head first, crushing his spine,
Christopher Reeve sits in an electric wheelchair.

The generator allows his respirator to push,
push air from his mouth to his lungs and back out again.
In his head he writes a song:

Superman, Superman where are you now?
The lights are out but we don't know how.
One giant leap and the end is nigh.
Superman, Superman, you can't really fly.

Quietly Dizzy

Martha's face glows with perspiration.
There are rules about closeness with strangers
that Alex would do well to remember.
But tonight he remains blissfully ignorant.
Quietly dizzy.

Break

We pause to look at these people, the city and its surroundings – water, suburbs, the way you pronounce *catastrophe* like it's the last word you will ever say. The onliners suffer tonight. Forced to break the habit of a chat room: *Nice to meet you.* The veil of a screen. It's time to decide what to reveal: *I work for myself. I don't get out much. I am a little complicated right now. I like stuff.* The fiction and the imagination. The stranger waiting in the dark alleyway. The delete button. The wit of your typeface. Delete. The monologue from the other side of the table. Delete. The hand on the subway. Delete. The scream at the amusement park. The straightest back. Delete. The hero in the distance. The buildings, torn down and replaced with lightweights. The old man dancing in the bar, pretending to be with the someone he loved. Serious. Business. Easily deleted. There, there she goes. The woman with the boy, the brave, brave boy. The letter torn up. The letter deleted. There, there it goes.

The Day

It was always going to come gently
rolling over again
into her room.

On a nice day for a walk.
Rose will pick up litter on her street
or write notes to the neighbours.

In a few days she'll tell stories about this and in the coming years
she'll say: *I was there* and *I did something* and it will be
one of those stories where everyone nods in appreciation.

And unless she wanted it to
she never really thought
it would stay dark forever.

She never really thought
she'd disappear into it.

And climbing stairs was easier then.
It reminded her to tread carefully over those awkward things
she'd recently said.

It reminded her to think of others
and what would happen.
What would happen if she fell.

About a Bridge

From the window,
the Williamsburg bridge stands unchanged.
The lights are not required.

Two coffee cups
and a plate of un-toasted bread
sit on the counter.

The focus changes each time Martha
blinks in and out. Above and under
the sky and steel.

The fridge smells like cheese
and onions. There is noise, but not much.
Scratching. Traffic. Footsteps.

This morning is not served with breakfast radio.
No traffic reports and clichés about sport
or soft rock, a bass beat for a love song.

She inspires levels in him.
A certain distance increasing
with each wave of sunlight on the water.

In Camera

With his own camera, Alex is forced into a photograph.
He hates this kind of stuff. Being an image.
A design.
Martha has ideas. She tells him to *act normal*
which he thinks is an *oxymoron*.
Are you calling me a moron?
He does a variety of things: scratches the surface of his stubble,
discards food from the freezer.
Acting normal. Acting like this woman is supposed to be here,
in his kitchen, as if they are together or something.
Acting. She kisses him on the back of his neck.
Quiet. Close by, someone talks about brilliant stars
and a new beginning. Far away. He's acting as if he is far.
Very far away. Only two weeks later, he wants this moment
as a poster. As a teaser for something a bit more real.
The immaculate still.
Ignorant of the fact that living things move.

Game

Now the kid from the Upper East
can finish his computer game.
Older guys from other countries
have passed him in the ranks.
Enemies stuck in mazes.
Hiding in dark corners.
On the porch, teenagers eat.
Gelato starts to refreeze, never as soft as before.
On screen, blood falls on blades of grass.

Strings Attached

Martha picks up her bag from the kitchen floor
and slings it on her shoulder. They hug.
She asks for his number.
I'll even give you my real number.
She says: *See ya later* and emerges into a Brooklyn street.

Far from home. Two strangers pass and she asks for directions.
West, the answer. *You are west.*
Let her construct a map and move
through straight lines and crosses. Aim a compass at the sun
to help direct her footsteps on the bitumen. Let her go.
See Martha walk towards tall buildings.
Again as she returns to Manhattan.
Let her back into that colour. Those heights. That energy.
But easy does it. Slow her down.
Make her take her time. Distract her with something
Wait. Stop. You!
as he considers running after her.
Behind you, behind you.
She turns.
She turns to the blank street. As still as today's breeze.
As still as sidelines. His image. As still as he sits.

It was really good
to meet you, Alex.
Thanks for ignoring
all the rules.

Alex Takes It On

Summer still, and nothing really changes.
Alex rides on the subway.
The headlines are all over the darkness.
Now he must learn a new way of reading.
The one where he puts himself into it.

Today, people walk a little slower.
They smile as if they've shared the last round of drinks
before the bar closed. Alex walks the streets.
His shoes soft on the sidewalk. Careful not to step on cracks.
The smell of stale beer.
The whir of machines making all the food we need to survive.
Alex checks his change. He buys a coffee.
Everyone he speaks to comments on the dark
and what happened to them. Stories and anecdotes.
Alex climbs the stairs. Only because he can.
The smells in stairwells never change.
Even between decades. They just never change.

Alex knocks on the door. Soon, she will open it.
Between the door and the frame, soon,
she will appear in backlight.
Bigger than a city. Ready, now.

Good to meet you too.
I'll call when things
calm down a little.

Questions

The place is more cluttered than Alex remembers.
In the kitchen, Rose flusters. Small talk follows about work
and of course, the blackout. About why and how and when
they would find out exactly why the power failed.

Money, computer crashes and politics follow.
At least, they agree, it's not the unthinkable.
Planes. Crashing.

And wasn't it clean? she says. *So clean.*
Like we'd all wiped our hands with disinfectant.

Still, his room is as he left it in '86. Models of buildings
on the shelves and posters of models on the walls.
Tanks remain parked in cupboards
and planes landed years before.
He's been saying for years that he'll
pack up his childhood in boxes and bags.
Letters written on the backs of magazines.
Superman and the soldiers hide out in dusty drawers.

That afternoon, over a cup of tea:
And did you stay in last night, Ma?

Oh, how I though of you all night. I did. Yes, I did.

Inventory, 2003

Above the tunnels and tracks
the concrete absorbs heat from the August sun.
Summer remains for now. It shocks and offends.

Now, people think carefully
about choosing a window seat.
It's harder to exit a plane, bus or train from there.

No one was rescued by Superman.
You forgot to ask for his help.
It's not like you needed him anyway.

The book, half written,
sits on the computer screen.
The people become fictional. They talk like characters.

Insurance forms sit on in-trays
on desks in office blocks.
The intern files by last names, rearranging the alphabet.

Candles, burned down
to the last speck of wick,
make hard puddles of wax on carpeted floors.

Elevators travel up and down,
the way they are supposed to.
Numbers pressed with hesitation.

People ring old lovers to see how they are.
They trade anecdotes filled with clues.
They can't help but ask: *Were you alone?*

The earth turns a little, summer heads
to the other side. People think about coats already.
Autumn leaves fall.

And when you wake,
in the dead hours of a dark night
whisper thoughts to the person sleeping next to you . . .

or write them down and send them off.
And if your speech bubble is blank, walk the city
to catch the thoughts of strangers wafting by.

As intimate as whispering.

Epilogue

This is something Alex invented: a helmet with lights that flash, but only when somebody else thinks of you. A light comes on and you think: *I wonder who could be thinking of me right now.* And you think: *SHE is thinking about me*, and then HER light goes on and she thinks: *HE* (but not you) *must be thinking about me* and so it goes, on and on and off again. *Whisper thoughts through the city.* People would wear their helmets in the city. Everywhere. While sleeping. Yes, even sleeping. And a man there, walking with his lights out until someone takes pity and thinks: *I should be thinking about you – somebody should be thinking about you. I'm going to think about you.* And one light in a helmet full of unlit lights starts to flash. They say they flash in Manhattan. Also, in Brooklyn . . . *Oh, how I though of you all night. I did. Yes, I did.*

Notes From the Author

Every Time You Close Your Eyes explores issues of real and imagined fear and the way the culture and society of New York changed between 1977 and 2003. I've been attracted to this theme and setting since spending time in North America in 2004 and listening to stories of the blackouts from Americans who lived through them. To explore the differences further, I spoke to Nancy Learner and Noel Rodriguez Jr., both citizens of New York City in 1977 and 2003. I am eternally grateful for their honest accounts of the events, moods and politics surrounding both blackouts. I would also like to acknowledge James Goodman's *Blackout* (2003) for further information.

The phrase 'Every time you close your eyes' is taken from the song 'Rebellion (Lies)' by Arcade Fire. Not entirely incidentally, their song 'Neighbourhood #3 (Power Out)' was inspired by a weeklong blackout in Montreal in 1988. PJ Harvey's song 'You Said Something' also features in this book.

Years have passed since the first word of this book was written and I owe a debt of gratitude to many people, far too many to name here. I will single out just a few.

Thanks to all at Wakefield Press, especially Michael Bollen, Clinton Ellicott and Angela Tolley. To my excellent friend Sonja Dechian who read and re-read countless drafts of this book, always questioning why and how and never allowing me to fall into laziness. Gratitude also goes to Ken Bolton who curates the Lee Marvin Readings in Adelaide. Many of these poems were first shared there and it was a privilege to lean on such a platform. Thanks to Jill Jones and Phillip Edmonds from the University of Adelaide who provided encouragement and support throughout the drafting of the book; and to Darren O'Donnell who insisted that I take it further. Finally, my love always to Rachel Petersen who appeared two thirds through the writing of this, and most thankfully never left.

Wakefield Press is an independent publishing and
distribution company based in Adelaide, South Australia.
We love good stories and publish beautiful books.
To see our full range of books, please visit our website at
www.wakefieldpress.com.au
where all titles are available for purchase.

Find us!

Twitter: www.twitter.com/wakefieldpress
Facebook: www.facebook.com/wakefield.press
Instagram: instagram.com/wakefieldpress